Take a trip down memory lane with this look back at 1976. America marks its 200th birthday with coast-to-coast celebrations, *Charlie's Angels* comes to TV and women everywhere want "Farrah Hair," Jimmy Carter is elected as the 39th President of the U.S., and 14-year-old Nadia Comaneci becomes the first gymnast to be awarded a perfect score of 10 in an Olympic gymnastic event. Remember the stories, photos, news, people, advertisements, sports and events that made 1976 your special year!

A walk back in time...

To:

From:

Managing Editor • Art Worthington

Publishers • Lawrence Siegel & Art Worthington

Cover Design • Peter Hess

Designer • Liz Howard

Writing & Research • Liz Howard

Facilitator • Pamela Thomas

.com

(800) 541-3533

AMERICA'S BICENTENNIAL

AMERICAN REVOLUTION BICENTENNIAL
1776-1976

Surrender at Saratoga 1777 by Trumbull
US Bicentennial 13 cents

SPIRIT OF 76

All the President's Men • The Ascent • Assault on Precinct 13 •
Bound for Glory • Buffalo Bill and the Indians, or Sitting Bull's Hist
Wash • Casanova • Cousin, Cousine • A Cricket in the Ear • De
Party • Dr. Black, Mr. Hyde • The Enforcer • Face to Face • Fam
Told Me To • The Gumball Rally • Gus • Harlan County USA • He
Be 25 in the Year 2000 • The Judge and the Assassin • The Killi
The Last Tycoon • Leadbelly • Lipstick • The Little Girl Who Live
Marathon Man • A Matter of Time • The Memory of Justice • M
Jugs & Speed • Murder by Death • Network • Obsession • The C
Again • The Ritz • Robin and Marian • Rocky • Rosy Dreams • S
The Shaggy D.A. • The Shootist • Silent Movie • Silver Streak • T
the Magic Flute • The Song Remains the Same • A Star Is Born
The Tenant • To the Devil a Daughter • Two-Minute Warning •

at the

MOVIES

by Blue Marine • The Bad News Bears • The Big Bus
Lesson • Bugsy Malone • Burnt Offerings • Carrie   Car
Hero • Diary of the Dead • The Divine Nymph • Don's
Plot • Freaky Friday • The Front • Futureworld • God
f Glass • Hot Potato • J.D.'s Revenge • Jonah Who Will
f a Chinese Bookie • King Kong • The Last Hard Men
wn the Lane • Logan's Run • The Man Who Fell to Earth
ay • Mikey and Nicky • The Missouri Breaks • Mother,
n • The Outlaw Josey Wales • The Pink Panther Strikes
stiane • Seven Beauties • The Seven-Per-Cent Solution
Slipper and the Rose • Small Change • The Smurfs and
tay Hungry • Storm Boy • Swashbuckler • Taxi Driver
ante Force • Voyage of the Damned • Welcome to L.A.

Oscars® Presented in 1976
for 1975 films

Best Picture
One Flew Over the Cuckoo's Nest

Best Director
Milos Forman, One Flew Over
the Cuckoo's Nest

Best Actor
Jack Nicholson, One Flew Over
the Cuckoo's Nest

Best
Actress
Louise Fletcher,
One Flew Over the Cuckoo's Nest

Best Supporting
Actor
George Burns,
The Sunshine Boys

Best Supporting Actress
Lee Grant, Shampoo

Best Song
"I'm Easy," Nashville

Best Picture
Rocky

Best Director
John G. Avildsen,
Rocky

Best Actor
Peter Finch, Network

Best Actress
Faye Dunaway,
Network

Best Supporting Actor
Jason Robards,
All the President's Men

Best Supporting Actress
Beatrice Straight,
Network

Best Song
"Evergreen,"
A Star Is Born

1976 Advertisement

If you have a kid like Mikey, you need a cereal like Life.

Even if your child is a picky eater like Mikey, he'll love Life Cereal, like Mikey.

Kids just seem to go for that oatsy, nutsy, downright crunchy taste.

So let the Mikey in your family try a bowl of Life. It's the delicious, high-protein cereal. From Quaker.

TOP GROSSING FILMS OF 1976

1.	Rocky	$117,235,147
2.	A Star Is Born	$80,000,000
3.	All the President's Men	$70,600,000
4.	The Omen	$60,922,980
5.	King Kong	$52,614,445
6.	Silver Streak	$51,079,064
7.	The Enforcer	$46,236,000
8.	Carrie	$32,211,330
9.	Family Plot	$23,770,000
10.	Marathon Man	$21,610,000

Sylvester Stallone and
Talia Shire star in *Rocky*

on television

PRIMETIME LINEUP
1976–77 Fall Schedule

		7:00	7:30	8:00	8:30	9:00	9:30	10:00	10:30
SUNDAY	ABC	Cos		The Six Million Dollar Man		ABC Sunday Night Movie			
	CBS	60 Minutes		The Sonny & Cher Show		Kojak		Delvecchio	
	NBC	The Wonderful World of Disney		NBC Sunday Mystery Movie: Columbo/ McCloud/McMillian & Wife/Quincy, M.E.		The Big Event			
MONDAY	ABC	Local	Local	The Captain and Tennille		ABC Monday Night Football			
	CBS	Local	Local	Rhoda	Phyllis	Maude	All's Fair	Executive Suite	
	NBC	Local	Local	Little House on the Prairie		NBC Monday Night at the Movies			
TUESDAY	ABC	Local	Local	Happy Days	Laverne & Shirley	Rich Man, Poor Man Book II		Family	
	CBS	Local	Local	The Tony Orlando and Dawn Rainbow Hour		M*A*S*H	One Day at a Time	Switch	
	NBC	Local	Local	Baa Baa Black Sheep		Police Woman		Police Story	
WEDNESDAY	ABC	Local	Local	The Bionic Woman		Baretta		Charlie's Angels	
	CBS	Local	Local	Good Times	Ball Four	All in the Family	Alice	The Blue Knight	
	NBC	Local	Local	The Practice		NBC Movie of the Week		The Quest	
THURSDAY	ABC	Local	Local	Welcome Back, Kotter	Barney Miller	The Tony Randall Show	The Nancy Walker Show	The Streets of San Francisco	
	CBS	Local	Local	The Waltons		Hawaii Five-O		Barnaby Jones	
	NBC	Local	Local	Gemini Man		C.P.O. Sharkey	Chico and the Man	Van Dyke and Company	
FRIDAY	ABC	Local	Local	Donny & Marie		The ABC Friday Night Movie			
	CBS	Local	Local	Spencer's Pilots		The CBS Friday Night Movies			
	NBC	Local	Local	Sanford & Son	Chico and the Man	The Rockford Files		Serpico	
SATURDAY	ABC	Local	Local	Holmes & Yoyo	Mr. T and Tina	Starsky and Hutch		Most Wanted	
	CBS	Local	Local	The Jeffersons	Doc	The Mary Tyler Moore Show	The Bob Newhart Show	The Carol Burnett Show	
	NBC	Local	Local	Emergency		NBC Saturday Night at the Movies			

new on the tube

The Bionic Woman

Family

Charlie's Angels

Family Feud

Laverne & Shirley

What's Happening!!

1 Happy Days

2 Laverne & Shirley

3 The ABC Monday Night Movie

4 M*A*S*H

5 Charlie's Angels

6 The Big Event

7 The Six Million Dollar Man

8 The ABC Sunday Night Movie

9 Baretta

10 One Day at a Time

11 Three's Company*

12 All in the Family

13 Welcome Back, Kotter

14 The Bionic Woman

15 The Waltons

16 Little House on the Prairie

17 Barney Miller

18 60 Minutes

19 Hawaii Five-O

20 NBC Monday Night at the Movies

* Debuted March 1977

1976 Advertisement

television's top 20
1976 - 77

On the Radio

Saturday Night Bay City Rollers
Convoy C. W. McCall
I Write the Songs Barry Manilow
Theme from Mahogany Diana Ross
Love Rollercoaster Ohio Players
50 Ways to Leave Your Lover Paul Simon
Theme from S.W.A.T. Rhythm Heritage
Love Machine The Miracles
December, 1963 The Four Seasons
Disco Lady Johnnie Taylor
Let Your Love Flow The Bellamy Brothers
Welcome Back John Sebastian
Boogie Fever The Sylvers
Silly Love Songs Paul McCartney & Wings
Love Hangover Diana Ross
Afternoon Delight Starland Vocal Band
Kiss and Say Goodbye The Manhattans
Don't Go Breaking My Heart
Elton John & Kiki Dee
You Should Be Dancing Bee Gees
(Shake, Shake, Shake) Shake Your Booty
KC and the Sunshine Band
Play That Funky Music Wild Cherry
A Fifth of Beethoven
Walter Murphy & The Big Apple Band
Disco Duck Rick Dees & His Cast of Idiots
If You Leave Me Now Chicago
Rock'n Me Steve Miller Band
Tonight's the Night Rod Stewart

Music Notes

New Bands

- Black Flag
- The Clash
- The Cure
- Foreigner
- U2

Bands Disbanded

- The Allman Brothers Band
- The Band
- Deep Purple
- Grand Funk Railroad
- Ike & Tina Turner

This Year's Biggest Hits

Dancing Queen
ABBA

Bohemian Rhapsody
Queen

If You Leave Me Now
Chicago

Fernando
ABBA

Notable Debut Albums
(in the U.S.)

Tom Petty and the Heartbreakers (self-titled)

Blondie (self-titled)

Boston (self-titled)

Ramones (self-titled)

Dreamboat Annie
Heart

Grammy Awards

presented February 19, 1977

Record of the Year
Tommy LiPuma (producer) &
George Benson, *This Masquerade*

Album of the Year
Stevie Wonder, *Songs in the Key of Life*

Song of the Year
Bruce Johnston (songwriter) & Barry
Manilow (performer), *I Write the Songs*

Wonder

Best New Artist
Starland Vocal Band

Best Country Vocal Performance, Female
Emmylou Harris, *Elite Hotel*

Best Country Vocal Performance, Male
Ronnie Milsap, *(I'm a) Stand By My Woman Man*

Best Country Vocal Performance by a Duo or Group
Amazing Rhythm Aces, *The End Is Not in Sight*

Best Pop Vocal Performance, Female
Linda Ronstadt, *Hasten Down the Wind*

Best Pop Vocal Performance, Male
Stevie Wonder, *Songs in the Key of Life*

Best Pop Vocal Performance by a Duo, Group or Chorus
Chicago, *If You Leave Me Now*

Best R&B Vocal Performance, Female
Natalie Cole, *Sophisticated Lady (She's a Different Lady)*

Best R&B Vocal Performance, Male
Stevie Wonder, *I Wish*

Best R&B Vocal Performance by a Duo, Group or Chorus
Billy Davis Jr. & Marilyn McCoo, *You Don't Have
to Be a Star*

1976 Advertisement

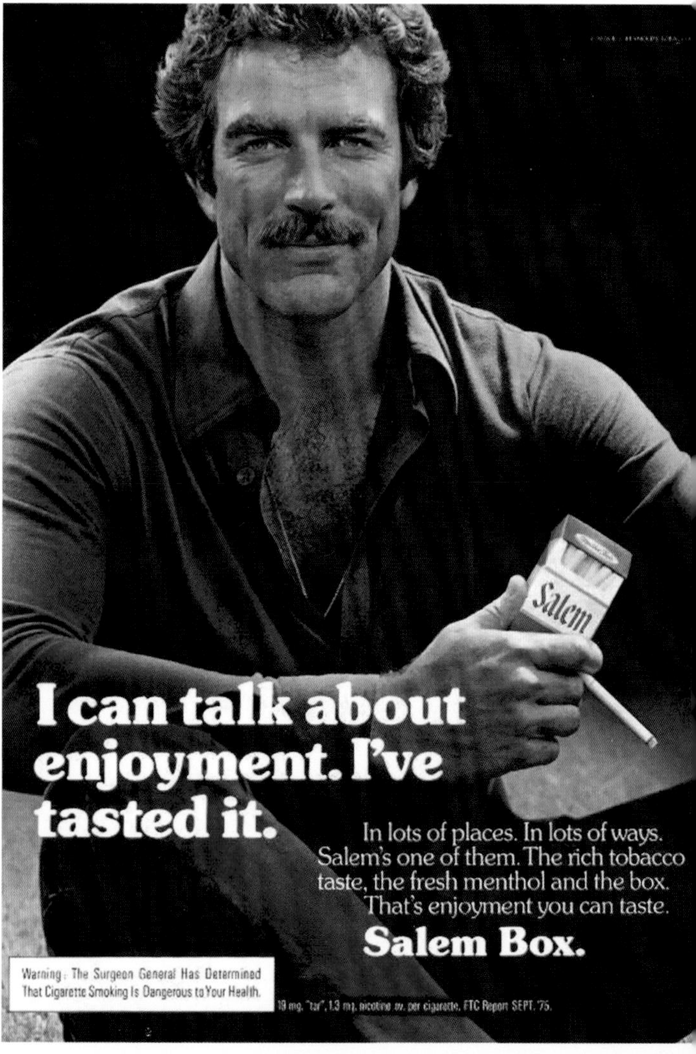

I can talk about enjoyment. I've tasted it.

In lots of places. In lots of ways. Salem's one of them. The rich tobacco taste, the fresh menthol and the box. That's enjoyment you can taste.

Salem Box.

18 mg. "tar", 1.3 mg. nicotine av. per cigarette, FTC Report SEPT. '75.

LITERATURE

The **NOBEL PRIZE IN LITERATURE** is presented to **Saul Bellow** of the United States

"for the human understanding and subtle analysis of contemporary culture that are combined in his work."

Interview with the Vampire, **Anne Rice**'s first novel in *The Vampire Chronicles*, a series of books featuring the vampire Lestat, comes out in April.

Alex Haley publishes *Roots: The Saga of an American Family*. It will be made into a popular television miniseries in 1977.

Jaws author **Peter Benchley** publishes his second novel, *The Deep*.

PULITZER PRIZES

PUBLIC SERVICE:
ANCHORAGE DAILY NEWS, *for its disclosures of the impact and influence of the Teamsters Union on Alaska's economy and politics.*

NATIONAL REPORTING:
JAMES RISSER, Des Moines Register, *for disclosing large-scale corruption in the American grain exporting trade.*

INTERNATIONAL REPORTING:
SYDNEY SCHANBERG, The New York Times, *for his coverage of the Communist takeover in Cambodia, carried out at great risk when he elected to stay at his post after the fall of Pnom Penh.*

POETRY:
JOHN ASHBERY, *Self-Portrait in a Convex Mirror*

HISTORY:
PAUL HORGAN, *Lamy of Santa Fe*

BIOGRAPHY OR AUTOBIOGRAPHY:
R. W. B. LEWIS, *Edith Wharton: A Biography*

FICTION:
SAUL BELLOW, *Humboldt's Gift*

Between March and June this year the towns of Spiro, Oklahoma, Brown wood, Texas and Jordan, Iowa are each hit by F5 (wind speeds of 261-318 mph) tornados. In each case damage to the town is extensive, and in Jordan nearly every building is destroyed, but there are only two casualties.

In March two explosions occur two days apart at the Scotia Mine in Kentucky, killing 26 miners.

In Italy at the Cavalese ski-resort, an aerial tram cable car falls 700 feet down a mountainside, killing 42 of the 43 occupants. Later, an automatic safety system that would have prevented the accident was found to have been turned off.

On September 10th two planes collide in the sky near Zagreb, Yugoslavia. Between British Airways Flight 476 and Inex-Adria Aviopromet Flight 550 there are 176 people onboard and all are killed due to mistakes made by air traffic control.

On October 6th Cubana Flight 455, en route from Barbados to Jamaica, is destroyed midair by two bombs planted by anti-Castro Cuban terrorists. All 76 lives onboard are lost.

On the Mississippi River just before dawn on October 20th the MV *George Prince*, a car and passenger ferry, is hit by the Norwegian tanker SS *Frosta*. The ferry is nearing its destination when the tanker sounds its horn, but it's too late and the ferry is broadsided, quickly submerges and is dragged under the tanker. Of the 96 people onboard 78 are killed.

1976
DISASTERS

On February 4th at 3:01 a.m. a 7.5 earthquake rocks Guatemala.

Some 23,000 lives are lost in the 39-second quake, and another 7

6,000 people are injured.

In May a 6.5 earthquake kills 976 people and leaves 70,000 homeless near Friuli in northeastern Italy.

The Tangshan earthquake occurs July 28th in China. The 7.8 (USGS later downgrades it to a 7.5) quake lasts 15 seconds and is followed

later in the day

by a major aftershock. The entire city of Tangshan is destroyed and the death toll is approximately a quarter million people.

An 8.0 earthquake in the Philippines near the island of Mindanao on August 16th sends a huge tsunami across the region within minutes of the quake, devastating some 430 miles of coastline. The combination of the earthquake and tsunami kills an estimated 8,000 people.

Where's the Little Dutch Boy *When You Need Him?*

In southeastern Idaho on the Teton River, an earthen dam that is finished in November 1975 fails spectacularly on June 5th, killing 11 people. The new reservoir is just about filled to capacity when water begins seeping through the dam, a fairly normal occurrence with earthen dams. At 7:30 on the morning of the 5th, the seepage turns into a muddy leak, and by two hours later the dam's embankment begins to erode from the water leaking out. Although bulldozers try to staunch the flow of muddy water they are unsuccessful, and by 11:15 the word goes out to evacuate the towns below the dam. The gap continues to expand and the bulldozer crews are forced to flee. At 11:57 the dam is completely breached and a third of its face has collapsed, sending over 200,000 cubic feet of muddy water rushing downstream. The towns of Wilford and Sugar City are particularly hard-hit, and Salem, Hibbard and Rexburg suffer damage as well. The dam cost the government approximately $100 million to build and over $300 million in claims related to the failure.

76 Presidential Campaign

THE GRIN WILL WIN
JIMMY CARTER PRESIDENT in '76

GIMME JIMMY
VOTE DEMOCRATIC

JIMMY '76

Jimmy
PRESIDENTIAL
CAMPAIGN HEADQUARTERS

Carter for President

BETTY FORD for FIRST LADY in '76

President Ford '76

REPUBLICAN 1976
FORD DOLE

because innocence is sexier than you think.

Love's Baby Soft® is that irresistible, clean-baby smell, grown-up enough to be sexy. Its soft-smelling, Pure and innocent. It may well be the sexiest fragrance around.

Love Cosmetics

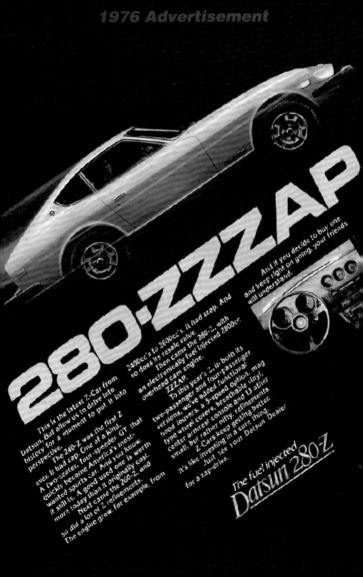

280-ZZZAP

This is the latest Z-Car from Datsun. But allow us to delve into history for a moment to put it into perspective.

The 240-Z was the first Z ever. It had zap. One of a kind. A two-seater, four-speeder GT that quickly became America's most-wanted sports car. And you know, it still is. A good used one is worth more today than it originally cost.

Next came the 260-Z, and so did a lot of Z refinements. The engine grew, for example, from 2400cc's to 2600cc's; it had zap. And so does its resale value.

Then came the 280-Z, with an electronically fuel injected 2800cc overhead cam engine. ZZZAP.

To this year's Z, in both its two-passenger and four-passenger versions, we've added functional hood louvers, a 5-speed option, mag type wheel covers, breathable vinyl, center armrest console and 13 other small, but rather nifty, refinements.

Z-Cars keep getting better. It's like investing in a sure thing.

And if you decide to buy one and keep right on going, your friends will understand.

Just see your Datsun Dealer for a zap-drive.

The fuel injected *Datsun* 280-Z

Across the country in small towns and big cities alike, America's Bicentennial, the 200th anniversary of the Declaration of Independence, is celebrated. As part of the Bicentennial celebration, on Thomas Jefferson's 233rd birthday the United States Treasury Department reintroduces the two-dollar bill.

Richard J. Daley, who was the mayor of Chicago for 21 years, dies in December.

Thirty people are injured when some 2,000 students at Escambia High School in Florida are involved in a race riot.

PRESIDENTIAL ELECTIONS

Jimmy Carter wins the Iowa Democratic Caucus. In July Carter is nominated for president at the Democratic National Convention.

Incumbent **Gerald Ford** edges out **Ronald Reagan** to win the Republican Party presidential nomination in August. On November 2nd Jimmy Carter is elected president of the United States.

The Supreme Court rules that the death penalty is a constitutionally acceptable form of punishment.

How to make your husband ask for Tuna Casserole.

Make it with Tuna Helper® and Bumble Bee® Tuna.

Here's a hearty main dish casserole that even the most stubborn meat and potatoes buff will go for — Tuna-Cheese Casserole with a buttered crumb topping. Tuna Helper makes it wonderfully easy to fix, and what makes it extra-special is Bumble Bee chunk light or solid white tuna, with its delicate taste and tender flaky texture. Look for other delicious recipes on the backs of Tuna Helper packages.

® Reg. T.M. Tuna Helper — General Mills, Inc.
®Reg. T.M. Bumble Bee — Castle & Cooke, Inc.

Tuna-Cheese Casserole Recipe

1 package Tuna Helper mix for noodles, cheese sauce'n tuna
2½ cups boiling water
1 can Bumble Bee Tuna, chunk light (6½ oz.) or solid white (7 oz.), drained
1 cup dairy sour cream
Buttered crumbs (below)
Snipped parsley or parsley flakes

Heat oven to 400°F. Mix Noodles, Sauce Mix, water, Bumble Bee tuna and sour cream in ungreased 2 quart casserole. Bake uncovered 25 minutes, stir. Sprinkle Buttered Crumbs around edge of casserole; top with parsley. Bake 5 minutes. Let stand a few minutes before serving. 5 servings.

Buttered Crumbs: Heat 1 tablespoon butter or margarine in 8-inch skillet until melted. Stir in ¼ cup dry bread crumbs. Heat over medium heat, stirring constantly, until bread crumbs are slightly toasted.

IN THE HEADLINES
1976

Cuba adopts a new constitution, the Socialist Constitution of 1976, in February.

In the central business district of Melbourne, Australia, the Victoria Club is robbed of between $6 million and $12 million. No one is ever convicted of the crime.

On August 26th the husband of Queen Juliana of the Netherlands, Prince Bernhard of Lippe-Biesterfeld, resigns as inspector-general of the Dutch armed forces and various other posts when it is revealed he accepted a $1.1 million bribe from Lockheed Corporation.

The first chief minister of the Turks and Caicos Islands, James Alexander George Smith "Jags" McCartney, is sworn into office August 30th.

On September 6th Lt. Viktor Belenko, a Soviet Air Force pilot, lands his MiG-25 jet fighter on the island of Hokkaidō, Japan and requests political asylum in the United States.

The Caribbean country of Trinidad and Tobago severs its links with the British monarchy, replacing Queen Elizabeth II with a president as its head of state.

WORLD

AFRICA

The president of **Nigeria**, General Murtala Mohammed, is assassinated in a military coup led by Lt. Col Buka Suka Dimka. He is succeeded by the chief of staff, Supreme HQ Olusegun Obasanjo.

On February 26th the Spanish Armed Forces withdraw from **Western Sahara**. The following day Western Sahara declares independence and the day after that Spain gives up its territories in Sahara, retaining the enclaves of Melilla and Ceuta.

Resentment builds among black students in Soweto, **South Africa** as a result of being forced to learn in a 50-50 mix of Afrikaans and English, a 1974 decree. At the end of April children begin to go on strike, refusing to go to school. An action committee is formed and a June 16th rally is organized. What starts off as a peaceful protest soon becomes deadly when police begin firing into the crowd of students and they begin to riot. Some accounts claim between 200 to 600 people died in the riots, but the official government death toll is 23.

EVENTS

ASIA

The totalitarian communist Pol Pot regime establishes a new constitution that goes into effect January 5th, and the Khmer Republic is officially renamed **Democratic Kampuchea**. In April Prince Norodom Sihanouk is forced to resign as head of state of Kampuchea and is placed under house arrest by the Khmer Rouge.

In Beijing, **China** huge crowds gather at Tiananmen Square in April to commemorate the passing of Premier Zhou Enlai, who passed away in January. A police crackdown removes flowers and poems left by the crowds and closes the square to the public.

One of the most influential figures in modern world history, **China**'s Chairman Mao Zedong dies on September 9th. In October Hua Guofeng is named Zedong's successor.

The Socialist Republic of **Vietnam** is created on July 2nd when North and South Vietnam unite.

In **Thailand** students gather at Thammasat University in protest of the return of Field Marshall Thanom Kittikachorn to Thailand. Police are called in and told to open fire on the protesters. For several hours police brutalize, humiliate and kill students. By the end of the attack 46 protesters lay dead and over 100 are injured.

Super get-together:

Your great van ideas and Ford's.

Ford changes van history—again! Ford's new-design Econoline is the only van with engine forward for extra room inside. With strong, separate frame/body construction. With power choices from 300 Six to 351 and 460 V-8's. With slick options like swiveling Captain's Chairs. Whatever your van ideas, Ford starts you out ahead!

Van shown has custom paint and wheels and tires added locally.

93 out of 100 of all Ford Trucks registered in the last 12 years are still on the job.

FORD

FORD DIVISION

WORLD

EUROPE

Raymond Barre becomes prime minister of **France** when Jacques Chirac resigns.

The president of **Ireland**, Cearbhall Ó Dálaigh, resigns when Minister for Defense Paddy Donegan publicly calls him a "thundering disgrace," and is succeeded by Patrick Hillery.

Northern Ireland's Constitutional Convention is dissolved in March and direct rule from London is put into action.

James Callaghan becomes prime minister of the **United Kingdom** in April after Harold Wilson's March resignation.

The **U.K.** and **Iceland** finally reach an agreement that the U.K. will no longer fish in the disputed waters off Iceland, and the Cod Wars end.

Due to metal fatigue the chiming mechanism on **England**'s Big Ben is destroyed on August 5th. It takes 9 months to rebuild.

In June **Poland**'s government plan to increase the price of basic commodities including food by as much as 100% is met by public protests, demonstrations, rioting and looting. The increasingly violent demonstrations last for seven days, after which the plan for a price hike is dropped.

EVENTS

WORLD

MIDDLE EAST

In **Lebanon** the civil war heats up in January when the PLO attacks Damour, destroying the buildings, killing around 600 Christian civilians and forcing the rest to flee. In June **Syria** switches its backing in the war, now opposing the Palestine Liberation Organization whom it had previously supported. Strong criticism of Syria from the Arab world follows the attack of East Beirut's Tel al-Zaatar refugee camp and the massacre of some 2,000 Palestinians by Christian forces, using arms supplied by Damascus. The U.S. ambassador to Lebanon, Francis Meloy, is assassinated in June, prompting the evacuation of close to 300 Westerners from Beruit. Even with the criticism of Syria, when the Arab League forms the Arab Deterrent Force to quell the fighting, it is made up of mostly Syrian troops, who occupy Lebanon in October and instill an uneasy truce in the war.

OTHER AREAS

Bangladesh and **Pakistan** establish full diplomatic relations.

Trying to control population growth, **India** enacts a measure changing the minimum age for marriage to 21 for men and 18 for women.

EVENTS

WORLD

NORTH AMERICA

José López Portillo succeeds Luis Echeverría as president of **Mexico**.

In Toronto, **Canada** the CN Tower is opened to the public. At 1,815 feet the communications and observation tower is the tallest freestanding structure on land in the world, a record it will hold for the next 31 years.

In October over one million Canadian workers stage a one-day strike protesting wage and price controls.

SOUTH AMERICA

The Dirty War escalates when a right-wing coup d'état overthrows **Argentina** president Isabel Perón on March 24th. A military junta headed by General Jorge Rafael Videla, Admiral Emilio Eduardo Massera and Brigadier Orlando Ramón Agosti seizes power and will remain in control until 1983.

Beginning in November 1975 and continuing this year is Operation Condor, a campaign of repression involving assassinations and intelligence operations by the governments of **Argentina**, **Chile**, **Uruguay**, **Paraguay**, **Bolivia** and **Brazil**.

EVENTS

SHASTA BRIGHTENS THE HOLIDAYS LIKE NO OTHER SOFT DRINK.

Put sparkle into any holiday party with Shasta. 14 great tasting flavors...each in Regular and Sugar-Free Diet. Cola, Draft Root Beer, Orange, Lemon-Lime, Strawberry, Ginger Ale, Black Cherry, Creme Soda, Cherry Cola, Grape, Red Apple, Grapefruit, Wild Raspberry, Tiki Punch.

In March 22-year-old **Patricia Hearst**, granddaughter of wealthy publishing mogul William Randolph Hearst, is convicted of a 1974 bank robbery and sentenced to 35 years in prison. Hearst is released from prison when her sentence is commuted by President Carter in 1979, and will receive a full pardon from President Clinton in 2001.

Serial killer **Ted Bundy** is convicted for the 1974 kidnapping of Carol DaRonch and sentenced to 15 years in Utah State Prison. Bundy is a suspect in a murder case in Colorado and is extradited there to stand trial. He escapes from a Colorado jail in December 1977 and goes on to kill 3 other women, as well as attack and severely injure 3 more before his arrest in February 1978.

Sara Jane Moore is sentenced to life in prison for the attempted assassination of President Ford in 1975.

In New York City **David Berkowitz**, aka **Son of Sam**, begins his killing spree, shooting two women on July 29, killing one of them. In October he shoots a couple sitting in a parked car; both survive. His last assault in 1976 occurs in November when he shoots two young women; both survive but one is paralyzed.

Bundy

Berkowitz

No matter how much your feet perspire, Sportwick socks will help keep them dry.

We make Sportwick socks for just about every sport. In the latest colors and styles. Still, the real beauty of our socks is how dry they keep your feet.

Take these Sportwick tube socks, for instance. Thanks to an exclusive patented process, they direct the perspiration *away* from your feet and into the socks' outer layer. So Sportwick socks never feel damp and clammy against your skin. No matter how much your feet perspire.

Sportwick socks by Interwoven. You might say they make giving a top performance no sweat. At least, from the knees down.

Sportwick by Interwoven

Hello...

Jennifer
Capriati

Colin
Farrell

Soleil Moon
Frye

Melissa Joan
Hart

Oliver
Hudson

Lil'
Kim

Keri
Russell

Fred
Savage

Alicia
Silverstone

Reese
Witherspoon

Goodbye...

Agatha
Christie

Ray "Crash"
Corrigan

J. Paul
Getty

Howard
Hughes

Dalton
Trumbo

Hughes

New in 1976

☆ The first commercial flights of the Concorde take place on January 21st as British Airways flies from London to Bahrain and Air France from Paris to Rio simultaneously.

☆ In Washington, D.C. the first 4.6-mile stretch of the Metro subway opens.

☆ Steve Jobs and Steve Wozniak form the Apple Computer Company, releasing the first Apple computer, the Apple I, on April Fools' Day.

☆ In Annapolis, Maryland the first female class is inducted at the United States Naval Academy.

☆ The first African American Secretary of the United States Army, Clifford Alexander, Jr., is confirmed.

☆ The United States government takes control of 13 Northeast railroads that have filed for bankruptcy and forms Conrail, a government-owned and-operated railroad.

☆ Farrah Fawcett's hairstyle sparks a trend for millions of young women, which lasts for nearly a decade.

☆ IBM introduces the world's first laser printer, the IBM 3800.

☆ New Jersey legalizes gambling casinos in Atlantic City starting in 1978. Governor Brendan Byrne makes it clear that the Mafia's influence in Nevada at casinos won't be tolerated in his state and declares, "The mob is not welcome in New Jersey!"

SCIENCE

1976

At a dedication ceremony on September 17th in Palmdale, California the first space shuttle, *Enterprise*, is rolled out in front of a crowd that includes most of the original *Star Trek* cast.

The Cray-1, one of the world's first supercomputers, is installed at the Los Alamos National Laboratory.

The first LAGEOS, Laser Geodynamics Satellite, is launched in May.

On July 20th the *Viking 1* lands on Mars, and on July 25th it snaps the famous Face on Mars photo. On August 7th *Viking 2* enters Mars' orbit and lands on the planet on September 3rd. *Viking 2* takes the first

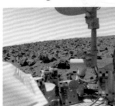

close-up color pictures of the planet.

In one of the most exciting discoveries of the 20th century the first megamouth shark is discovered when it becomes tangled with a U.S. Navy ship anchor off the coast of Oahu, Hawaii.

MEDICINE

1976

The American Legion convention held in Philadelphia, Pennsylvania at the Bellevue Stratford Hotel in July is attended by more than 4,000 members and family. Just a few days after the start of the convention people begin to fall ill with flu-like symptoms. Some 221 people are reported ill, and when 34 of them die from pneumonia Americans prepare for an epidemic. The swine flu is first suspected but is soon ruled out when the feared epidemic fails to materialize. Within six months the cause is isolated to a bacterium, *Legionella pneumophilia*, that had been spread by the hotel's air conditioning system, making these the first recorded cases of Legionnaires disease.

The first reported cases of the Ebola hemorrhagic fever occur in Sudan between June and November and another outbreak occurs in Zaire (now the Democratic Republic of the Congo) in September and October. The Sudan strain has a mortality rate of 50%, whereas the Zaire strain has a mortality rate of nearly 90%. Between the two outbreaks there are 602 confirmed cases amd 431 people die. The incubation period is between two days and three weeks, the onset sudden, characterized by high fever, and death or the road to recovery occurs in six to ten days. There is no specific treatment and no vaccine currently exists.

BRECK GIRL

Julie Ann Forshee
of Fayetteville, Arkansas

As proudly American as any
1776 patriot, Julie represents
1976 young women
as America's Junior Miss.

Beautiful Hair Begins with
GOLD FORMULA BRECK SHAMPOO
Three special formulas — for Dry Hair — for Normal Hair — for Oily Hair.

1976 NOBEL PRIZE WINNERS

PEACE

Betty Williams *and* Mairead Corrigan

for their work as a cofounder of Community of Peace People, an organization dedicated to promoting a peaceful resolution to The Troubles in Northern Ireland.

Williams

Corrigan

PHYSIOLOGY OR MEDICINE

Baruch S. Blumberg *and* D. Carleton Gajdusek

for their discoveries concerning new mechanisms for the origin and dissemination of infectious diseases.

Blumberg

Gajdusek

PHYSICS

Burton Richter *and* Samuel Chao Chung Ting

for their pioneering work in the discovery of a heavy elementary particle of a new kind.

Richter

Ting

CHEMISTRY

William Lipscomb

for his studies on the structure of boranes illuminating problems of chemical bonding.

Lipscomb

Fashion

1976 WINTER

O L Y M P I C S

The XII Olympic Winter Games are held February 4-15 in Innsbruck, Austria.

Hamill

Austrian Franz Klammer wins the men's downhill alpine skiing match in 1:45.73.

American Dorothy Hamill wins the gold in figure skating. Her "wedge" haircut inspires a craze that sweeps the nation.

West German skier Rosi Mittermaier dominates the women's alpine skiing events with two golds and one silver, just missing a third gold by 0.13 seconds.

Winning their fourth straight ice hockey gold medal is the USSR men's hockey team.

Canada refuses to compete in ice hockey for the second consecutive Olympics.

MEDAL COUNT (TOP 5 GOLD)	GOLD	SILVER	BRONZE	TOTAL
Soviet Union	13	6	8	27
East Germany	7	5	7	19
United States	3	3	1	7
Norway	3	3	1	7
West Germany	2	5	3	10

1976 SUMMER OLYMPICS

MEDAL COUNT (TOP 5 GOLD)	GOLD	SILVER	BRONZE	TOTAL
Soviet Union	49	41	35	125
East Germany	40	25	25	90
United States	34	35	25	94
West Germany	10	12	17	39
Japan	9	6	10	25

The Games of the XXI Olympiad are held July 17 - August 1 in Montreal, Canada.

14-year-old Romanian gymnast Nadia Comaneci is the star of the show when she earns seven perfect 10.00 scores, winning three golds. Since 10.00 scores had been considered unobtainable, the score board can only accommodate a three-digit score, so her scores show as 1.00.

U.S. track and field athlete Bruce Jenner wins the gold medal for the decathlon with a world record of 8,634 points.

Japanese gymnast Shun Fujimoto performs on a broken knee, helping win the gold medal for the team championship.

Comaneci

WE'RE LOOKING FOR PEOPLE WHO LOVE TO DRIVE.

We realize that, for some of you, driving an automobile is about as exhilarating as riding an escalator. That's sad.

Because with the right kind of car in your hands, the act of driving can be one of the truly pleasant things you do each day.

Which brings us to Camaro. In fact it brings lots of us to Camaro.

People who love to drive love Camaro because it's definitely a driver's car. It sits low and stands wide and moves like it really means it. Camaro is quick, quiet, tight and tough. All of which translates to a very special "feel". The spirit of Camaro. The lift the car can give you, even just driving to work.

If you love to drive, or would like to, take a turn in a '77 Camaro one day real soon.

Your Chevy dealer has one all gassed up and ready to go.

Driving gloves are optional.

Chevrolet

CAMARO

Baseball

In the American League Championship Series it is the New York Yankees over the Kansas City Royals 3-2, and for the National League champions it's the Cincinnati Reds who beat the Philadelphia Phillies 3-0. The Reds sweep the World Series 4 games to 0.

The National League takes the All-Star Game on July 13th at Veterans Stadium, 7-1, and George Foster is the game's MVP.

Ted Turner buys the Atlanta Braves.

Most Valuable Player
AL **Thurman Munson**, *Yankees*
NL **Joe Morgan**, *Reds*

Cy Young Award
AL **Jim Palmer**, *Orioles*
NL **Randy Jones**, *Padres*

Rookie of the Year
AL **Mark Fidrych**, Tigers
NL **Butch Metzger**, Padres, and **Pat Zachry**, Reds

Thurman Munson

Joe Morgan

Hockey

Going into the quarter finals for the 1975-76 season, it's the **New York Islanders** over the **Buffalo Sabres** 4-2, the **Boston Bruins** over the **Los Angeles Kings** 4-3, the **Philadelphia Flyers** over the **Toronto Maple Leafs** 4-3, and the **Montreal Canadiens** over the **Chicago Black Hawks** 4-0. In the semifinals the **Montreal Canadiens** face off against the **New York Islanders**, beating them 4-1, while the **Philadelphia Flyers** defeat the **Boston Bruins** 4-1. The **Canadiens** defeat the **Flyers** 4-0 and take home the Stanley Cup.

Prince of Wales Trophy
Montreal Canadiens

Art Ross Trophy
Guy Lafleur,
Montreal Canadiens

Bill Masterton Memorial Trophy
Rod Gilbert
New York Rangers

Calder Memorial Trophy
Bryan Trottier
New York Islanders

Hart Memorial Trophy
Bobby Clark
Philadelphia Flyers

Lady Byng Memorial Trophy
Jean Ratelle
Rangers/Bruins

NHL Plus/Minus Award
Bobby Clarke
Philadelphia Flyers

Vezina Trophy
Ken Dryden
Montreal Canadiens

Football

PRO BALL

In the 1976-77 football season the NFL expands to 28 teams with the addition of the Seattle Seahawks and the Tampa Bay Buccaneers.

The 1976 season ends with the Conference Championship Games and the Super Bowl being played in January 1977. On January 4th at the Oakland Coliseum the **Oakland Raiders** trounce the **Pittsburgh Steelers** 24-7 while at Metropolitan Stadium the **Minnesota Vikings** beat the **Los Angeles Rams** 24-13. Super Bowl XI is held January 9th at the Rose Bowl in Pasadena, California where the **Raiders** take home the title, defeating the **Vikings** 32-14.

The Associated Press NFL Player of the Year/Most Valuable Player Award goes to Chicago Bears running back **Walter Payton**.

COLLEGE BALL

Orange Bowl
Ohio State Buckeyes over Colorado Buffaloes
27-12

Cotton Bowl
Houston Cougars over Maryland Terrapins
30-21

Sugar Bowl
Pittsburgh Panthers over Georgia Bulldogs
27-3

Rose Bowl
USC Trojans over Michigan Wolverines
14-6

Heisman Trophy
Tony Dorsett, Pittsburgh Panthers

Eddie Robinson Award Coach Of The Year
Johnny Majors Pittsburgh

All college bowl games with the exception of the Sugar Bowl are played in January 1977.

Basketball

NBA

In the Western Conference semifinal games the Golden State Warriors beat the Detroit Pistons 4-2, and the Phoenix Suns beat the Seattle Supersonics 4-2. Meanwhile in the Eastern Conference it's the Boston Celtics over the Buffalo Braves 4-2, and the Cleveland Cavaliers over the Washington Bullets 4-3. The Suns beat the Warriors 4-3 and the Celtics defeat the Cavaliers 4-2 for the conference finals. The season ends with the Celtics beating the Suns 4-2 for the NBA Championship. Game 5 of the series is widely regarded as one of the most exciting games in history when it goes into triple overtime with Boston winning 128-126.

NCAA

This year sees two undefeated teams, Indiana and Rutgers, enter the tournament. In the Final Four Michigan beats Rutgers 86-70 and Indiana defeats UCLA 65-51. Coach Bob Knight takes Indiana all the way to the national title against Michigan, 86-68. This is the first time two teams from the Big 10 play in the title game.

Tournament's MOP
Kent Benson, Indiana

Tournament's Top Scorer
Scott May, Indiana (113)

PLAYER OF THE YEAR AWARDS

United Press
Scott May, Indiana

U.S. Basketball Writers Association
Adrian Dantley, Notre Dame

Rupp & Naismith
Scott May, Indiana

SPORTS SHORTS

AUTO RACING

Daytona 500:
David Pearson

Winston Cup:
Cale Yarborough

Indianapolis 500:
Johnny Rutherford

Top Fuel NHRA
Supernationals:
Shirley Muldowney

24 Hours of Le Mans:
Jacky Ickx and
Gijs van Lennep

GOLF

U.S. Open:
Jerry Pate

PGA Championship:
Dave Stockton

Masters:
Raymond Floyd

British Open:
Johnny Miller

LPGA Championship:
Betty Burfeindt

U.S. Women's Open:
JoAnne Carner

TENNIS

MEN'S:
Australian Open:
Mark Edmondson

French Open:
Adriano Panatta

Wimbledon:
Björn Borg

U.S. Open:
Jimmy Connors

WOMEN'S:
Australian Open:
Evonne Goolagong

French Open:
Sue Barker

Wimbledon:
Chris Evert

U.S. Open:
Chris Evert

Davis Cup:
Italy
over Chile

BOXING

World Heavyweight
Muhammad Ali
over Ken Norton

FIGURE SKATING

Men's Champion:
John Curry
Britain

Women's Champion:
Dorothy Hamill
United States

Pair Skating
Champions:
Irina Rodnina &
Alexander Zaitsev
Soviet Union

Ice Dancing
Champions:
**Lyudmila
Pakhomova** &
Alexandr Gorshkov
Soviet Union

CYCLING

Giro d'Italia:
Felice Gimondi
Italy

Tour de France:
Lucien Van Impe
Belgium

World Cycling
Championship:
Freddy Maertens
Belgium